Absurdity Abounds

Peter Bui

BookLeaf Publishing

Presentation by *BookLeaf Publishing*

Web: www.bookleafpub.com

E-mail: info@bookleafpub.com

ISBN: 9789357214940

First edition 2022

To my beloved sweetheart, Amber, without whom inspiration would never find me.

The Fool

Pass neither judgement nor pity upon the fool at the bar,
for I assure you, he is much more cunning by far.
By outward appearance, his antics are certainly hilarious
but beware of his plot, ever so nefarious.
Not so reckless as to be random,
but also not so particular to be personal,
and yet executed so exquisitely
you'd be right to assume rehearsal.
it'd be madness to think it anything but auspicious.
Such trustworthy treachery is a sight to behold.
Although shrouded behind a mask of oblivious oddity,
do not deny the darkness that is yet to unfold.
Not by his hands and not ever again
no, the winds have shifted direction, tonight
my beasties are starving, bloodlust matching his
and ready to rip and tear, slash and bite
unlike his grand entrance, he slips away as he leaves
and like a cheerful, new couple, his victim is in tow

but stopped in their tracks, they are met by me and my own
as innocent as he pretends, he and I both know
he is no longer the hunter,
and his sands are almost depleted
his smile quickly fades
for he knows he is defeated.
my beasts start their advance,
my shadow wolf at my side
lunges forward with fangs
as he attempts to run and hide.
it tears away at his legs
biting deep into the bone
and just like his victims past
he is left immobile and alone
My raven swoops down
and glares with a laugh and smile
as it plucks out his eyes and rips out his tongue
so he too cannot see or be heard for miles
and my final beast, he can only feel it surround him
does it slither or does it crawl?
is it one or is it many?
and what invasion shall he befall?
its weight is unbearable
and he can hardly catch his breath
he endures pure agony
and at the very moment of his death
he is filled with regret and sorrow

as he pleads and rues the day
that he ever chose play the fool
and end up as my prey.

Dreams

Beyond the veil of a slightly altered stream
I find reflection inside of a waking moment of serene
Daffodils and daisies fly along by,
reminding me of long past summer skies
Falling through the clouds and back towards peace
Without the slightest care or concern in the least
I'm coming home. I can feel it, ever so close
Hands stretched out towards what the soul wants most
And lifted on up to enjoy the warmth of the sun
Over towers, mountains, and even against the sky have I won
And on my victory lap down
I return to the ground
And from most peaceful sleep, I awaken, but then
I am left dreaming to dream the same dream once again.

Rest

Deep along an old wood, perched up upon a
branch
sat a very proud and young owl
pruning its feathers and enjoying the night
it was near a clearing with an odor most foul
it was protective of what laid at the ground
but knew that scavengers were on the prowl
the first to approach, was an older racoon
who had learned many lessons
and knew that it had come too soon
but still it had asked, for a small piece at least
but the owl shouted back,
"you monster, you beast!
how dare you look upon this as your own
feast?!"
And with the sound of the screech
the racoon went scuttling away
realizing it was right
that it was not the right day.

Next came a mother coyote
with pups not far behind
all of them starving
and very excited for this find
but as she attempted to take her prize

the owl boomed with a fearsome cry
"you monster! You Beast!
How dare you disrespect me so this night?"
"Proud owl, I meant no disrespect,
but my children are starved
I guarantee your honor,
and that I meant you no harm."
"I do not accept your excuse
and offense I still take
this is not a meal
I shall allow you partake."
and though its screeching proved ineffective
at scaring the mother away
its dive and its talons towards the pups
spoke louder than anything the owl could say.

The dawn was nearing,
and the time for the owl to rest was at hand
but then came the last one
a young human
The owl puffed up its feathers,
and readied its claws
it absolutely refused to lose
to a breaker of laws
it roared with a ferocity unmatched by all
"You monster! You Beast!
How dare you even approach
you violator of nature, I can stand you the
least!"

the young human stepped no further
but let out a sad sigh
looked up at the owl
before giving a kind smile
"Good owl, proud owl, oh majesty of wisdom
I only meant to honor you, not make you a feast
to turn you into art
to immortalize you, at least."
The owl thought for a moment
its watch could finally cease,
"perhaps that is not a bad way
for me to rest eternally in peace."

Home

It is not the depths of the unknown that give me a fright
It is not the pride of victory that pushes me to fight
I care not for prestige or title or even immortality
I only seek what is base for all of humanity
not just comfort nor simply a shelter
more than a place to eat and lie my head
not simply a place to build a family
that I can pass onto after I'm dead
it is where I can dare to dream
and look upon with unmatched inquire
where the impossible can find as much possibility
as it may so much desire
a place that knows me
far more than I know my own mind
and a place that can protect me
as I leave my demons behind
so perhaps a home is not a place at all
and yet still makes me feel like I belong
gives me the will to wake up
and makes me feel strong
so as it turns out

I do have a home, as it were
as a matter of fact I always will
so long as I have her.

Lost Hope

Madness consuming
the rage within blooming
it's spilling and oozing
yet I'm hardly moving
chaos is ensuing
don't know what I'm doing
the effort is grueling
keep on misconstruing
the lie from the true thing
my hope keeps renewing
you'd think it'd be soothing
but I am the fools' king
forever, it's looming
the judgement the ruling
the ending appears to be out of my choosing.

A Fictioner's Memoir

Illusory worlds guide me steadily
towards a mind that continues to weigh on me heavily
a shattered mirror, a monster in sight
and yet this cool summer breeze still calms me tonight
unyielding, unwieldly, utterly relentless
caught up in a storm of unending repentance
a spectre, a ghoul, an entity of dark
reaches out, it clutches onto my sad, little heart
snips away at the strands holding the stitching together
what it looked like before, I can hardly remember
whoever's reality this is by design
I can assure you, it most certainly is not mine
I merely exist, in some bastardization of the process
yet it is all naught but mimicry, I must fully confess
lost between worlds, lost in a daze
trapped deep within an ouroboros maze
sinking into madness, past the point of no return
you'd think I'd be better... you'd think I'd have learned

The Mosquito

Flying on wings of one that has fallen,
her dark heart is amplified by her intention
my body and soul filled with apprehension
her cold bite robs me of my very essence
her presence
is still so very near
I hear
I hear her next to my ear
but then she is gone, onto her next batch
leaving me with nothing,
save for an itch I cannot scratch.

Nightmares

Crickets chirp
I can't sleep
It's not from the heat
of the bedsheets
it's not the ticking of the clock
or the random object that dropped
I hear the swirling of the fan
the squeal of dead silence
trying to figure out as hard as I can
but none of that is keeping me up
it's not from the tea I drank
I'm not staring into the night sky
maybe...yeah...maybe I do know why...
I guess I'm just afraid
or so it would seem
maybe I'm just terrified
of having another bad dream.

Perspective of Madness

To live in the shadows
to live in the dark
to live with an empty
empty heart
at a loss of words
from the immense pain
at a loss of honor
he can never regain
oh how the jester does his skit
and how the joker has such wit
he laughs, "ha ha!" in the face of death
even if it be, from dragon's breath
with such darkness in him
he is still such a fool
you'd wonder why
he's not that cruel
but then you see his goofy smile
and then you realize all the while
that though his life is all hell and dread
it all depends on what's in your head.

Second Home

A light breeze blows through the trees
and surrounds me with a sense of serenity
beyond compare and beyond what I would dare
to attempt to grasp or find
I find
that a place as simple as this
could somehow still bring such bliss
such wonderment, and oh the life!
to be surrounded by so much
fills me with such joy, such awe
that it's difficult to leave and withdraw
and although it is not really a place
anyone should ever truly own
I can't help but see the forest
as a place I can call home.

A Beautiful Rainy Day

The trickling of the summer rains
soothes my soul
with a song that sings
straight into its core
to sit in the rain
with that single one
what more,
what more
could anyone ask for?
oh how perfect it would be,
to share a moment in the rain
to close our eyes
to feel that spray
until we wash all of the calamities away
maybe then a storm
may not be a storm
but rather...our own
kind of beautiful day.

Delight in Madness

Welcome, my dear victims, come one, come all!
fall deep into insanity within my madness carnival!
leave behind, what you thought was once true and held dear
and perhaps learn to enjoy yourself with a little taste of fear
dance with my puppets,
let their strings bind you close
and ignore all the reality
you held within you the most
mind not the lion, the tiger, nor the bear
pay much more mind to the red eyed hare
as it juggles and hops along with the tune
with fur as white and shines like the moon
do not be afraid to become a full loon
in fact enjoy your new insanity cocoon
you may find, in fact, it serves as a boon
when the lad dressed as cupid shoots at you, his harpoon
let it reel you in
accept your new crown
be the star of the show,
my glorious new clown!

Wonderland of Delights

Strawberry jelly cookies with a vanilla crème
colorful cupcakes with a bright candy gem
chocolate mousse with a mint leaf and its stem
tapioca pudding and its subsequent mayhem
maple syrup drizzle upon a small pecan tart
caramel glass strings make croquembouche an art
piled high macarons seem like a good place to start
pistachio gelato has a strong grip on my heart
white hot cocoa to warm a cold soul
goes well with a fluffy matcha cake roll
sour candy drops test your control
fresh kettle corn, I could eat a whole bowl!
artfully iced sugar cookies served on a plate
heavenly powdered beignets are well worth the wait
sticky toffee puddings with cream and dates
strawberry rhubarb pie, I dare not hesitate
apple strudel with a wonderfully flaky crust
spiced carrot cake is an absolute must
tres leches topped with a cinnamon sugar dust
a warm peach cobbler is the one that I trust
whipped cheesecake that is as light as air
royally enjoy red wine poached pear

whatever you choose, just be fully aware
that which you enjoy was made with love and
care

Eternity...in Progress

Tick tock...tick tock
is the sound I hear
as I listen to the clock
as it whispers through the seams
just as if it were a dream
or at least... so it would seem
If only time
would just slow itself down
just enough for me to wish
as the star flies by
far off into the sky
I cannot finish
as I lay here tonight
The words of my dream
that float within my mind
They remind...
...me
of a faint echo in my heart
that I have long since left behind
but what is it? This sound...
like forgetting something that I found
or to be locked within a prison
with no chains to keep me bound
I am well prepared to take flight
with no destination in sight

and no wings to fly away
and yet here I need not stay,
and...try as I may
I want not otherwise anyway
What game is this I play?
how much more will I run
'Til I be done with this maze
Years? Months? Maybe days?
or will the hands of the clock
show me their mercy at last?
Have I any time left?
Or...has that time already past?

Seasons of Joy

The wonder of winter keeps my heart alight
the lights all around to enjoy through the night
and if there is snow, I just may, I just might
play outside all day to my heart's delight
the symphony of spring brings about a new
song
nature comes awake for all to sing along
life comes renewed where its always belonged
proving to us that it does, indeed, go on
the soul of the summertime gives us pause for
some rest
or find new worlds along an adventurous quest
the fruits of our labor are enjoyed at their best
and celebrations abound with our most
colorfully dressed
the autumn harvest season gives us comfort
above all
the leaves give us a dance along as they fall
we give thanks to the spirits as we heed their
call
and provide for everyone, whether big or small.

Vampyre

Drawn into the night, as I have abandoned the day
I have cast out the light and its comforts away
left to be a creature of the dark
left to hone my newly acquired art
to sate my new hunger
to keep myself younger
I now walk along the path of shadow
I no longer belong to the surface, although
I find comfort amongst my fellow creatures of the night
as we rule over the fear in the hearts of those who deem themselves right

Dark Masquerade

Dance along this waltz I play
Dance all night into the day
Melt into the words I sing
Fall into my everything
Leave behind the world you knew
Join a life built just for you
Find the joy your heart desires
and let it take you home

Trust in me, you won't be lost
Follow me through any cost
Do not fret, the way is clear
I will protect you from what you fear
never again, will you know harm
I am here, don't be alarmed
Hold me close, hold me now
I'll never let you go

Now you're safe and warm inside
You no longer have to hide
See the life you get to live
See the comfort that I give
There's no one else that you will need
no other law that you must heed
stay with me until the end
my one and only friend.

The Moon is Smiling Tonight

The Moon is smiling tonight
and the stars, they shine so bright
even the clouds
are dancing around
and the wind it sings a song aloud

The Moon is smiling tonight
I wanna hold you close and tight
The trees they sway
hip, hip, hooray!
The night's my favorite time of day

Oh, the Moon is smiling tonight
Rest your head and close your eyes
I love you so
and bid you a good night.

Imaginarium

Come along with me to find imagination
unleashed into the cosmos of endless creation
where limits and chains bound us not
where inspiration and magic is all we've got
hold fast to nothing
let your heart be set free
let wonder guide you
to where you are most meant to be
joy and sorrow hold equal import in your heart
every little experience must play its set part
but there is no one path
for which you must take
you are free to choose your own way,
make your own mistakes
but I assure you, at the end,
what you see shall be true
for the visage you shall see
is undeniably you
do not be hindered by what others have said
it matters very little when all are dead
so let the majesty of existence
be a making of your own
for the art that you create
is yours, and yours alone.

www.ingramcontent.com/pod-product-compliance
Lightning Source LLC
Chambersburg PA
CBHW051756130826
49812CB00033B/1174
* 9 7 8 9 3 5 7 2 1 4 9 4 0 *